THE AMERICAN CAUSE

ARCHIBALD MACLEISH

THE AMERICAN CAUSE

DUELL, SLOAN AND PEARCE

NEW YORK

first edition

PRINTED IN THE UNITED STATES OF AMERICA

BY QUINN & BODEN COMPANY, INC., RAHWAY, N. J.

CONTENTS

FOREWORD

FOREWORD

HERE as in other countries the opponents of fascism have been obliged to make their way, not against the fascists, but against those whom the fascists would destroy. At the beginning, in the Spanish War, when the question of fascism was the question of the fascist purpose, the opponents of fascism were obliged to make their way against the Best People and against the news services upon which the Best People depend. The Best People, here as in England and in France, preferred to believe that fascism—particularly fascism in Spain—was a bulwark against bolshevism and a protection of the status quo. And their news services supported them in that belief. The small group of writers and reporters and ambulance drivers and plain citizens who protested that fascism, including fascism in Spain, was precisely what the fascists said it was, were written off as fellow-travelers of the communists. . . . Until the communists switched over to the fascist side, when they were written off as dupes.

Now, five years later, when the question of fascism has become the question of the defense of the United States, the opponents of fascism are obliged to make their way against a larger opposition—the opposition of the people of good will, the peaceful citizens who hope by hating force to have no need to face it. The peaceful citizens, persuaded by the reactionaries of the right and left and by a sprinkling of discouraged liberals, refuse again to hear the facts. They prefer to believe that fascism, though it may be fascist revolution to the Spaniards and to the Austrians and to the Czechs and to the Poles and to the Danes and to the Norwegians and to the Dutch and to the Belgians and to the French and maybe to the British, is nothing to the Americans but a revival of the War of 1914. And the writers and journalists and teachers and politicians who protest that fascism is still precisely what the fascists say it is are written off again. The only difference is that they are written off this time not as communists but as patrioteers: breeders of bloody passions: nationalists: war-mongers.

But abuse of the anti-fascists did not dispose of the fascist question in Spain and will not dispose of it here. The issue in Spain was not whether a group of anti-fascist writers here and in England and France were fellow-travelers of the communists. The issue in Spain was whether these writers were writing the truth when they said that the Spanish War was the beginning of a fascist revolution. And the issue now is not whether anti-fascist writers are chauvinists or war-mongers or whatever, but whether they are still writing the truth when they continue to say that fascism is revolution and that people who love freedom will either defend their freedom with an ardor equal to the ardor with which it is attacked or will see it disappear.

In a paper written before the fall of France and published in the *New Republic* on June 10 under the title "Post-War Writers and Pre-War Readers" I stated my own conviction that fascism is a faith which is no less powerful because it is a negative faith in obedience, in discipline, in brutality, in death; that a free people cannot fight fascism unless it believes with even greater conviction that freedom is good and can be attained and that slavery is evil and can be opposed; that unless we regain in this democracy the conviction that there are final things for which democracy will fight—unless we recover a faith in the expression of these things in words—we can leave our planes unbuilt and our battleships on paper, for we shall not need them.

I still hold that conviction, as the two papers here presented will, I think, make clear. I have no reason to hope that it is a conviction which will be shared by those who think the war in Europe is another "European War" which will touch us or not touch us as we choose. But for those who are willing to face the demonstrated fact that fascism is a revolutionary and entire attack upon the institutions and the culture and economy of democratic peoples, a revolutionary attack which has already destroyed these institutions over much of Europe and has declared its purpose to destroy them elsewhere—for those who are willing to face the recorded facts the conviction may have merit.

Citizens of an imperialistic, nineteenth-century world were wise to question publicists and politicians who talked about democracy and war. The wars they talked about were wars democracy could have avoided. But citizens of a world in which democracy is hunted down by fascism—citizens of the last great democratic power not yet bombed by fascist bombers—will think about democracy and war with other feelings. The war now threatened is a war no democratic nation can avoid by wishing to, but only by surrender or by standing ready to resist. And the declarations of a democratic faith are not incitements to make war but to resist it. Only if the democratic cause becomes a fighting cause which can resist attack if need be, will the democratic world survive.

A. MacL.

THE AMERICAN CAUSE

THE AMERICAN CAUSE

THE issue before the American people is not a political issue nor an issue to be decided by a public act. It is an issue between the American people and themselves: an issue which involves the vitality and the resources of the American soul.

These, I am well aware, are large and ornate words. They are words which a man would have used at the risk of his reputation for sincerity a dozen months ago. But they are words which none of us can help but use today. History, not rhetoric, has put them in our mouths. History has shown us at late last that the issue which divides our time is far more than an issue between armed forces. History has shown us that it is an issue between worlds: an issue which depends more surely on our souls than on our weapons:

an issue which no nation can avoid. Specifically and precisely, history has made plain to us a fact we had refused before to see—the fact that the enemy which attacks us attacks us not with planes alone or tanks alone or arms, but with violence of belief. And the issue which the people of this country face, the issue which lies between this people and itself, is the issue whether or not those who believe in democracy—those specifically who believe in democracy in the United States—can bring against the violence and fanatical obsession of that invading faith a stronger faith, a more resisting ardor of their own.

Before the Battle of France—a battle which may prove to have been more decisive in our own history than in the history of Europe—fascism had seemed to us a force of weapons driven onward by the fear of force behind. But in the Battle of France we learned, in the words of a manifesto issued by a group of the most distinguished scholars in this country, that the enemy "were stronger in arms because they were stronger in heart. It was their fanatical faith that gave them wings and fire. It was the singleness of their purpose that quickened the spearhead of their march." * In France also we learned that the weakness of the democracies—the weakness at least of the democracy which there fell—was not, as we had wished to believe, a weakness only in arms, only in mechanical contrivances. We learned, in the words of the same manifesto, that the blindness of democratic diplomacy and the helplessness of democratic strategy "were the external symptoms of a decay of the men. . . . This they called appeasement. It implied that no conviction is worth fighting for and that the boundaries between good and evil had fallen. Military defeat was the embodiment of moral abdication."

It was the Battle of France which posed the issue we now face. Before that battle we had thought ourselves spectators of a war in Europe.

* *The City of Man, a Declaration on World Democracy* (The Viking Press, 1940).

After it, we knew the war was not in Europe but nearer—in the darker and more vulnerable countries of men's hearts. And after it we were not certain it was we who were spectators.

But the Battle of France did more than pose this issue. It weighted it—and weighted it against us. Before the Battle of France we had not understood—as a nation we had not understood—that the vitality of our democratic faith was put in issue. After the Battle of France we feared the issue was already lost. We saw then that the war was not, as we had wished to believe, a war between European powers which wanted conflicting things but a war between human beings who believed conflicting things. We saw that the differences of belief were differences as to the kind of society in which men should live. We saw that those who believed in the kind of society in which we also believe had been opposed not only by weapons, not only by machines, but by other men who believed, and believed fanatically, in the total destruction of that society. We saw that in the fighting which followed it had been those who believed fanatically in destruction who had been stronger and those who believed in the society in which we believe who had been less strong—less strong not only in their weapons but in their devotion to their cause. And we had wondered. We wondered whether the sickness of democracy in France would prove to be the sickness of democracy in every country. We wondered whether democracy, which had been unable to match conviction with conviction and certainty with certainty in France, would be able to match conviction with conviction elsewhere. We still are wondering. We are wondering whether democracy in the United States has other spiritual weapons than the doubts and misgivings which ten years of depression and twenty years of skepticism provided for the men of France to fight with.

It is of this fear I wish to speak. And to speak as candidly and earnestly as I am capable of speaking. It is a fear which exists—and which exists in the minds not of foolish or of frightened people, but of responsible men who love this country as well as any of its people love it. It is also an understandable fear, for events which all of us have witnessed make it understandable. It is not a fear therefore which scornful men can put aside, or which demagogues can shout down, or which the patriotic societies can suppress with resolutions. It is a fear of which we must take account. But it is nevertheless—or so at least it seems to me—a fear both needless and mistaken. For it rests upon a total misconception of the democratic cause. It rests, to be precise, upon the misconception of democracy which those who most despise democracy have done their best to propagate and broadcast through the world. It is the fear of those who, being democrats themselves, accept the definition of democracy their enemies have written.

The enemies of liberty are not saboteurs in material things alone. They are saboteurs also in the things of the mind. And it is in the things of the mind that their sabotage is most dangerous. To destroy a machine or a manufacturing plant is one thing. The loss is great but the plant or the machine is replaceable. To destroy the integrity of words and to destroy the credibility of the users of words is another: neither can be replaced. The enemies of liberty, here as in other countries, practice the destruction of the integrity of words and the destruction of the credibility of the users of words. Indeed, it is this practice which principally characterizes the enemies of freedom in our time. They are the first men—the first men in the five hundred years since Johannes Gutenberg Zum Jungen, Knight of Mainz, invented the art of printing—the first men to use the printing press, deliberately and systematically, as an instrument of confusion and deceit. They are the first men in the five centuries of printing to turn the printing presses, like machine guns, on the people.

And nowhere have they used these Kulturwaffen to destroy a word more skillfully than with the word democracy—the word essential to our cause—the word which *is* our cause—the word we must defend whatever else we lose, or fail to fight for, or do not defend. What the enemies of liberty would have us take the word democracy to mean is not what Adams thought it meant, or Jefferson, or those who took it westward through the Shenandoah, or those who came to find it here by shipload after shipload through a hundred years. What the enemies of liberty would have us take the word to mean is something men and money and machines created in the nineteenth century and *called* democracy—a way of owning property, a scheme of doing business, an opportunity for comfort or for power or for certain forms of gain or entertainment.

It is this the enemies of liberty would have us take the word to mean. And it is with this meaning in our minds that they would have us make the choice before us—a choice, they say, between the new oncoming order of their fascist world and an old corrupted system full of fat and death—a choice between the new and iron cause for which a people can forget itself and sacrifice itself and go without and suffer and if need be die, and, on the other side, a world of goods and things and comforts and amusements with nothing to believe in but more goods, more things.

This was the choice which their confusions and their defamations and deceits presented to the citizens of France—and which the citizens of France, duped by confusions and deceits, accepted. It is the choice which many in this country, duped or themselves the dupers, would accept as well. The diplomat who tells us that democracy is dead in England, meaning by democracy a way of trading stocks, a chance to make ten millions in the market, accepts the choice the citizens of France accepted. The famous woman who assures us in a beautiful and cadenced prose that democracy is old in every country, and that the future like a wave will drown it down, accepts the same alternatives of terror and despair.

But the fears and desperations and defeats

which these and others like them breed and scatter are unreal fears. The democracy of which this writer and this statesman speak is not democracy but a distorted lie which both, but for their different reasons, take for true. Democracy itself has never been and is not now and never can become a way of trade, a world of goods, a heap of products, whether those products are of gold or steel or corn or silk or what-not: whether the trade is large or small or free or planned or neither. And only a very foolish man—only a man who had no understanding of the word democracy, or what it had been once, or what it can be—would take the issue in these terms and let his enemies compel him to defend, not the dream of freedom in the mind, not the way of freedom toward the future, but things already made, systems established, ways of trading, heaps of goods piled up.

If democracy is what the fascists say it is—if democracy is nothing but the world of innumerable automobiles and the best telephone system on earth and a new gadget just around the corner and the radios driveling on in the hotel lobbies eighteen hours out of twenty-four and the simpering legs in the magazine advertisements and the simpering voices on the movie screen and the hundreds of thousands of miles of roadside billboards with the billboard faces and the ten millions of unemployed waiting for the next boom—if democracy is only this, then democracy cannot survive attack, for democracy is not a cause that men will fight for.

But the true issue is not this issue; democracy is not the world that men and money and machines built in the nineteenth century and called democracy. The real issue is an issue to be fought in the hard and stony passes of the human spirit—the strict Thermopylaes of time where even if a man is killed he cannot die. And democracy itself is neither things nor goods nor fatness and indifference and an empty heart, but winter on the Massachusetts Bay and cold at Trenton and the gunfire in Kentucky and the hungry ground. The real issue is an issue between the frenzy on the one side of a herded, whipped-up, crowd-begotten "cause," and on the other side the single man's belief in liberty of mind and spirit; his willingness to sacrifice his goods and comforts and his earnings for its sake.

The democratic faith which swept the world—the democratic faith which men believed in and men fought for, the faith which men believe in and will fight for still, is not a faith in things or goods or fortunes. John Milton knew the democratic faith that men will fight for. He spoke of it not once but often:

"And as for you, citizens, it is of no small concern, what manner of men ye are, whether to acquire, or to keep possession of your liberty. Unless your liberty be of that kind which can neither be gotten nor taken away by arms (and that alone is such which springing from piety, justice, temperance, in fine from real virtue, shall take deep and intimate root in your minds) you may be assured that there will not be wanting one, who, even without arms, will speedily deprive you of what it is your boast to have gained by force of arms. . . . For know (that you may not feel resentment, or be able to blame anybody but yourselves), that as to be free is precisely the same thing as to be pious, wise, just and temperate, careful of one's own, abstinent from what is another's, and thence in fine, magnanimous and brave—so to be the opposite of these, is the same thing as to be a slave; and by the wonted judgment and as it were by the just retribution of God, it comes to pass, that the nation, which has been incapable of governing and ordering itself, and has delivered itself up to the slavery of its own lusts, is itself delivered over against its will to other masters—and whether it will or no is compelled to serve."

John Milton's democracy was a democracy in which men believed. It was a democracy for which a band of sober and unmilitary men fought as armies had not fought before them. It was a faith more powerful than any faith or cause which could be brought against it. It has been a faith more powerful than any other for three centuries of time and on two continents. It is still a faith more powerful than any other. All our history has made this plain. Whenever in the history of this nation we have given ourselves to the labor of creating upon this continent a life in which every man might have the freedom of his mind, we have been confident and certain of our future and assured and asked no questions either of ourselves or anyone. Whenever we have given ourselves to other labors, we have lost the meaning of our lives and lost our certainty and questioned everyone and most of all ourselves.

Three generations back in the thirties and the forties of the last century when the four-hundred-foot side-wheelers with the crystal chandeliers and the mahogany bars and the eight course dinners and the filigree funnels with their sparks like crazy stars went hooting and slapping up the Ohio and the Hudson and the Mississippi, the Americans had no questions about democracy. They had a job to do. They had the toughest job a people ever undertook—the job of clearing and settling and tying together with ships and roads and rails and words and names the largest area lived on as a single social unit by any nation, at any time. They had the job of creating on an undiscovered continent a country where a hundred million men could live in freedom from the rest and from each other. They had the actual and present job of clearing on this continent the quarter sections where a man could build his freedom out of logs and nails.

And while they had that job to do they asked no questions. They knew what democracy was. They knew what they were too. They were the smartest, toughest, luckiest, leanest, all-around knowingest nation on God's green earth. Their way of living was the handsomest way of living human beings had ever hit on. Their institutions were the institutions history had been waiting for. If you had told them anyone else had a harder hold on the earth than they had, or anyone else believed in himself more than they believed in themselves, they would have laughed in your face. And gone on with their working.

Who they were, what they were, never bothered the Americans. Virginia gentlemen and Boston philosophers and Long Island poets and visiting British lecturers might write and talk and wonder about American manners and American origins and American politics and the American soul. Americans didn't wonder. They knew all about them. They knew about origins. They had all the origins of Europe in their veins before the century was over—all the races a man ever heard of and a lot more beside. Races didn't bother the Americans. They were something a lot better than any race. They were a People. They were the first self-constituted, self-declared, self-created People in the history of the world. And their manners were their own business. And so were their politics. And so, but ten times so, were their souls.

Who an American was and what democracy was, was nothing to talk about. You could see for yourself. An American was a man who had the luck to be born on this continent where the heat was hotter and the cold was colder and the sun was brighter and the nights were blacker and the distances were farther and the faces were nearer and the rain was more like rain and the mornings were more like mornings than anywhere else on earth—sooner and sweeter and lovelier over unused hills.

An American was a man who knew which way to take to reach tomorrow. An American was a man who could let himself in and let himself out and nobody asking him "please" not even the President. An American was a man who never asked anyone anything—who he was or where he came from or what he did—because it was answer enough to be a man. At least in America.

That was the way it used to be in this country. That was the way it was while the people of this country were clearing the quarter sections for a free man's field. That is the way it has been whenever we have remembered clearly and understood with reality what democracy is.

For democracy is never a thing done. Democracy is always something that a nation must be doing. The quarter sections which were freedom a hundred years ago are now not freedom. Freedom will be somewhere else. But the labor of creating freedom is the same. And the consequence.

What is necessary now is one thing and one thing only—that the issue of democracy be made precise and clear—that democracy become again democracy in action, not democracy accomplished and piled up in goods and gold.

Democracy in action is a cause for which the stones themselves will fight.

THE AMERICAN MOBILIZATION

THE AMERICAN MOBILIZATION

MANY of those who have spoken and written of the mobilization of this country for defense assume that the mobilization which has been imposed upon us is a mobilization, not merely of arms, but of every resource, moral as well as material, of which the country can dispose. Upon that assumption they include, with weapons and with raw materials of war, the country's artists and its writers and their work.

It is an interesting assumption for two reasons. First, it assumes that the work of American artists and writers and musicians is a national resource, important enough to be mobilized along with men and arms, and, second, it assumes that the kind of mobilization which is now going forward in America is a mobilization in which the work of writers and artists has its proper part.

The first assumption will startle a considerable number of American painters and poets and musicians. They have not been aware for the last several decades that the nation felt an urgent need of their work. There has been talk of the arts and of letters as there is always talk of arts and letters, but the work of artists and writers—the work they are capable of performing for their contemporaries—their peculiar and proper work of interpreting the purpose of a generation to itself, has not been demanded of them. And for a very simple reason. Which is this: that their contemporaries have found the answers elsewhere.

For the better part of a generation the people of this country, like the people of other countries in the West, have found their explanations of their lives, and their interpretations of their experience, not in the work of their artists and their poets, but in the formulas and propositions and hypotheses which explain the nature of man and the pattern of his life in terms of the goods he uses and the products he requires. The Americans particularly have looked to these formulas and propositions for guidance in the interpretation of their history, the understanding of their present and their attempts to foresee their future. They have believed that they were closer to reality if they considered, not what they were, but only what they ate and wore. They have believed that they possessed their experience if they could express it in figures, and that their history was comprehensible if their history was written in terms of economic compulsion and the necessities of goods and trade. They have believed, finally, that those who interpreted life in graphs and statistical tabulations and the economic compulsions of which graphs and tabulations are the outward form, were the serious men, the intelligent men, the informed interpreters, and that all artists, and particularly novelists and poets, were marginal figures whose concern was with something not quite serious and not quite real.

It is not remarkable, therefore, that poets and painters should feel some astonishment today to see themselves and their work counted among the essential resources of their nation. Their astonishment, however, need not be unduly great. The inward life of a people, like the inward lives of the men and women who make up a people, has a slow and breaking rhythm, a long and almost imperceptible preparation like the preparation of a wave, and a sudden lifting, a sudden rushing forward. For a decade, for a generation, the thinking of a people will be fixed in certain forms, certain formulas, certain explanations which stand between the people and experience itself—the experience either of their own lives or of the artists who present the image of their lives. And then, suddenly, in due and inevitable course, the forms, the formulas, crumble against the obstacles of time and the life breaks forward.

It is this which has happened to the doctrine of economic infallibility in America today. The glassy wave of economic omniscience has stumbled against the rocks the economists forgot about, and the publicists and professors of economics are already complaining that poets have dared to raise their voices and to speak of things economists do not recognize as real. It is a curious fact, but a fact not without its ironic interest, that one of the elements the economists failed to count on was the capacity of the human heart for evil. The other was its capacity for good.

The rise of fascism, demonstrating as it did that men can be led by lies to desire slavery and death, demonstrated also that human motivation is not the simple thing the professors of economic doctrine affected to believe. And the fight against fascism, demonstrating that men will sacrifice their safety and their goods and every material advantage to defend a hopeless cause even in another country—and one thinks of Hemingway and Malraux and of Regler and of many others—the fight against fascism demonstrated, if demonstration was needed, that men are capable of generosities which no theory of materialism has ever yet explained or ever will. Even the Communist Party, which found in material causes the whole explanation of human conduct, has demonstrated by its own that there are certain deeds which men will do—surrender of principle and betrayal of cause among them—for no reason more material than fear.

The assumption, therefore, that the work of artists and of writers may again be needed in America can be accepted without undue reservation. The economic preconceptions, the brittle orthodoxies which stood between the writers and the artists and their people, are not as solid as they were. The second assumption, however, the assumption that the kind of mobilization now going forward in America is a mobilization in which the work of writers and of artists has its proper part, presents a greater difficulty. For if it is true that the American mobilization now in process is a mobilization which properly includes artists and writers and musicians, then it is a mobilization for a farther purpose and on a bolder scale than is commonly believed. It is a mobilization for something far, far greater than temporary defense against a temporary danger.

The mobilization of a people to meet and to ward off a temporary danger of attack is not an action which involves writers as writers, artists as artists. Such a mobilization is no part of the continuing life to which the artist and the writer belong, for it is no part of the continuing life of the people. It is, at the best, time out of that life to do a necessary and unpleasant job—time out to kill a snake—time out of the people's plans, time out of their hopes, time out of their lives—an interruption of every honest purpose and of every decent labor until the attacker is destroyed. Writers and artists and musicians have no place in it as writers and as artists and musicians.

Writers may join the ministry of propaganda, or sign up and keep their diaries in their duffle bags and maybe live to publish them, or suffer and remember afterwards and write the bitter unforgettable books of indignation and despair; and artists may paint the posters for the Red Cross or the national loans or try their hands at camouflage or carry a gun and die like Gaudier-Brzeska (and with him, as Pound said, there died a lot of first-rate sculpture); and musicians may play in the bands or write the official songs for the official sopranos from the Metropolitan or maybe, if they're lucky, "La Madelon," or maybe nothing, but there is no place in the plan for their own work—their own painting or their writing or their music.

The only mobilization of the resources of a democratic people which involves the writers and the artists as such—as themselves—is a very different mobilization. It is a mobilization of the people to defend themselves against attack not by interrupting their life as a people but by fulfilling their life as a people; not by defending against, but by living for; not by denying, whether with words or with guns, but by affirming. It is a mobilization of all the resources of a democratic people so that democracy may become itself and live, not only to survive this danger but to surmount it, and go forward, and go on beyond.

In such a mobilization the writers and painters and musicians of this country have a place as large as any. Their work is needed, not in some other form or shape, but in its own. For it is the simple truth that the mobilization of the possibilities of a free people is inconceivable without them. What a people can become is the accomplishment in act of what a people can conceive. What the people of a nation can conceive is what their artists and their poets can make actual to them and thus possible. It is the power truly to inhabit the present—the power to inhabit the possibilities of their own lives—which the poets of a people can confer upon them. And it is that power which the citizens of a people's country have need of at the great epochs of their history when, conscious of themselves, conscious of their necessities as a people, conscious of their destiny, they gather themselves to create again their future. The writers, the painters, the musicians who are part of such a mobilization of the resources of a nation may die in the end as other men may die, may suffer the loss of their work and be hurt, maimed, impoverished, but not as victims, not as men enlisted in another's cause. For the cause is their own. The cause is the creation of a future worthy of mankind.

Whether the mobilization of this country in the face of fascism is a mobilization of this second kind I do not know. But this I think I do know: that unless it is such a mobilization of every resource, every possibility of freedom, not to resist alone but to assert, and to become, and to fulfill, it cannot be successful. It cannot be successful *even as defense*. The danger which faces us is a danger so great, so terrible, so immediate, so close that only the re-creation of the people's will and the people's strength, only the realization of every possibility of the people, will enable the people's government to survive.

To mobilize planes only or armies only, forgetting our purposes as a democratic people, interrupting our history, neglecting the realization of our own hopes, is to invite disaster. Fascism does not attack with planes alone or with armies. Fascism as we now see, as we have now learned and will not again forget, fascism is an inward enemy which attacks within more dangerously than without, a revolutionary force which is not less terrible, but more terrible, because its end is ignorance and destruction. The collapse of France was a collapse from within, a collapse of will and conviction and belief; and the conquest of France was a conquest from within, a conquest of one purpose by another purpose. Fascism, whether we like it or not, is a cause; and only a fighting cause can conquer it. Democracy, to conquer, must become again a fighting cause. And democracy, which had not been a fighting cause for many years, which men here and in other countries have taken for granted, exploited for profit, turned into "business," democracy will not become a fighting cause if even the poor beginnings of democratic hope are interrupted and broken off, and war and weapons are its single aim.

Democracy as a fighting faith is faith in the freedom of the common people, faith in the capacity of the common people to create a world more human and more decent and more just than any world a tyrant or a demagogue or any so-called revolutionary party or any self-appointed aristocracy of wealth and talents can impose upon them. Democracy as a fighting faith is an affirmative faith, a faith in freedom for, not freedom from, a faith in the people's freedom to create their future for themselves. Those who think the Bill of Rights is all there is to democracy, those who think democracy is a private thing, an insulation from others, have failed to understand either their own or any other history. Democracy as a fighting cause is the cause to which Carl Sandburg gave a name: The People, Yes.

And mobilization for the defense of democracy in the face of the greatest danger which has ever threatened freedom must be the mobilization of every possibility the people have, not to defend themselves, not to resist, but to build higher and to build stronger the house of freedom on this ground: to create in America the thing so many men have dreamed of and have never seen—democracy itself—democracy in action. If the mobilization of America today is such a mobilization —and I hope it is—American writers and artists and musicians are a part of it. And if the mobilization of America is a mobilization of which its artists and its writers are a part, then the American cause is again the cause of the creative human spirit—the cause no enemy has ever overcome. Or ever will.

by Archibald MacLeish

THE HAPPY MARRIAGE

THE POT OF EARTH

NOBODADDY (A PLAY)

STREETS IN THE MOON

THE HAMLET OF A. MAC LEISH

NEW FOUND LAND

CONQUISTADOR

FRESCOES FOR MR. ROCKEFELLER'S CITY

UNION PACIFIC—A BALLET

PANIC (A PLAY)

PUBLIC SPEECH: POEMS

THE FALL OF THE CITY (A VERSE PLAY FOR RADIO)

LAND OF THE FREE

AIR RAID (A VERSE PLAY FOR RADIO)

AMERICA WAS PROMISES

THE IRRESPONSIBLES

THE AMERICAN CAUSE

Heath's Modern Language Series.

FRENCH GRAMMARS AND READERS.

Bruce's Grammaire Française. $1.15.
Clarke's Subjunctive Mood. An inductive treatise, with exercises. 50 cts.
Edgren's Compendious French Grammar. $1.15. Part I. 35 cts.
Fontaine's Livre de Lecture et de Conversation. 90 cts.
Fraser and Squair's French Grammar. $1.15.
Fraser and Squair's Abridged French Grammar. $1.10.
Fraser and Squair's Elementary French Grammar. 90 cts.
Grandgent's Essentials of French Grammar. $1.00.
Grandgent's Short French Grammar. 75 cts.
Roux's Lessons in Grammar and Composition, based on *Colomba*. 18 cts.
Hennequin's French Modal Auxiliaries. With exercises. 50 cts.
Houghton's French by Reading. $1.15.
Mansion's First Year French. For young beginners. 50 cts.
Méthode Hénin. 50 cts.
Bruce's Lectures Faciles. 60 cts.
Bruce's Dicteés Françaises. 30 cts.
Fontaine's Lectures Courantes. $1.00.
Giese's French Anecdotes. 00 cts.
Hotchkiss' Le Primer Livre de Français. Boards. 35 cts.
Bowen's First Scientific Reader. 90 cts.
Davies' Elementary Scientific French Reader. 40 cts.
Lyon and Larpent's Primary French Translation Book. 60 cts.
Snow and Lebon's Easy French. 60 cts.
Super's Preparatory French Reader. 70 cts.
Bouvet's Exercises in Syntax and Composition. 75 cts.
Storr's Hints on French Syntax. With exercises. 30 cts.
Brigham's French Composition. 12 cts.
Comfort's Exercises in French Prose Composition. 30 cts.
Grandgent's French Composition. 50 cts.
Grandgent's Materials for French Composition. Each, 12 cts.
Kimball's Materials for French Composition. Each, 12 cts.
Mansion's Exercises in Composition. 160 pages. 60 cts.
Marcou's French Review Exercises. 25 cts.
Prisoners of the Temple (Guerber). For French Composition. 25 cts.
Story of Cupid and Psyche (Guerber). For French Composition. 18 cts.
Heath's French Dictionary. Retail price, $1.50.

Heath's Modern Language Series.

ELEMENTARY FRENCH TEXTS.

Easy Selections for Sight Translation (Mansion). 15 cts.

Ségur's Les Malheurs de Sophie (White). Vocabulary. 45 cts.

French Fairy Tales (Joynes). Vocabulary and exercises. 35 cts.

Saintine's Picciola. With notes and vocabulary by Prof. O. B. Super. 45 cts.

Mairêt's La Tâche du Petit Pierre (Super). Vocabulary. 35 cts.

Bruno's Les Enfants Patriotes (Lyon). Vocabulary. 25 cts.

Bruno's Tour de la France par deux Enfants (Fontaine). Vocabulary. 45 cts.

Verne's L'Expédition de la Jeune Hardie (Lyon). Vocabulary. 25 cts.

Gervais Un Cas de Conscience (Horsley). Vocabulary. 25 cts.

Génin's Le Petit Tailleur Bouton (Lyon). Vocabulary. 25 cts.

Assolant's Aventure du Célèbre Pierrot (Pain). Vocabulary. 25 cts.

Assolant's Récits de la Vieille France. Notes by E. B. Wauton. 25 cts.

Muller's Grandes Découvertes Modernes. 25 cts.

Récits de Guerre et de Révolution (Minssen). Vocabulary. 25 cts.

Bedollière's La Mère Michel et son Chat (Lyon). Vocabulary. 25 cts.

Legouvé and Labiche's Cigale chez les Fourmis (Witherby). 20 cts.

Labiche's La Grammaire (Levi). Vocabulary. 25 cts.

Labiche's Le Voyage de M. Perrichon (Wells). Vocabulary. 30 cts.

Labiche's La Poudre aux Yeux (Wells). Vocabulary. 30 cts.

Lemaitre, Contes (Rensch). Vocabulary. 30 cts.

Dumas's Duc de Beaufort (Kitchen). Vocabulary. 30 cts.

Dumas's Monte-Cristo (Spiers). Vocabulary. 40 cts.

Berthet's Le Pacte de Famine. With notes by B. B. Dickinson. 25 cts.

Erckmann-Chatrian's Le Conscrit de 1813 (Super). Vocabulary. 45 cts.

Erckmann-Chatrian's L'Histoire d'un Paysan (Lyon). 25 cts.

France's Abeille (Lebon). 25 cts.

Moinaux's Les deux Sourds (Spiers). Vocabulary. 25 cts.

La Main Malheureuse (Guerber). Vocabulary. 25 cts.

Enault's Le Chien du Capitaine (Fontaine). Vocabulary. 35 cts.

Trois Contes Choisis par Daudet (Sanderson). Vocabulary. 20 cts.

Desnoyer's Jean-Paul Choppart (Fontaine). Vocabulary. 40 cts.

Selections for Sight Translation (Bruce). 15 cts.

Laboulaye's Contes Bleus (Fontaine). Vocabulary. 35 cts.

Malot's Sans Famille (Spiers). Vocabulary. 40 cts.

Meilhac and Halévy's L'Été de la St.-Martin (François). Vocab. 25 cts.